the Triumph of the Son

of the Son

(a paraphrase)

Bill Hunter
with Michael Hunter
illustrations by Charles Timothy Prutzer

Published by CSN Books
1975 Janich Ranch Court
El Cajon, CA 92019
Toll free: 1 (866) 484-6184
www.CSNbooks.com

1 2 3 4 5 6 7 8 9 10

To Him who is able to do immeasurably more
than all we ask or imagine,
according to His power that is at work within us,
to Him be glory in the church and in Christ Jesus
throughout all generations, for ever and ever! Amen.

Ephesians 3:30 (NIV)

author's note

"The form of Hebrew poetry is that
of thought-rhyme, parallelism of
members and verses, not of sound."
Erich Sauer, *The Dawn of World Redemption*

Applying Sauer's definition, this is a poem of Hebrew tradition – the same tradition from which the Old Testament was written.

> Don't journey quickly.
> Read slowly.
> Chew and digest.
> Taste and enjoy.

This book is not important because of the word of the writer, but because it gathers pivotal events from the Words of the Master.

This book is a paraphrase of the defining moments of Biblical history, focusing on choices made and the consequences of those choices—what Oswald Chambers calls the "parenthesis of life." As Chambers says, "if you want to understand the (A)uthor, pay particular attention to the parenthesis." History is shaped by the choices made and the consequences of those choices.

- when Adam and Eve ate of the other tree.
- when Cain slew his brother.
- when Noah devoted his life to the ark.
- when Abraham took his journey of faith.
- when Moses became the lawmaker and the deliverer.
- when David learned to love God above all and became the Father's favorite lionkiller.

Their decisions have played out in history from the day of their defining choices.

And then came the One
the Son of God
the Man Christ Jesus
the King of Kings
the Deliverer of us all.

His choice to do the Father's will, even at the cross, spared us from the consequences of our sins and delivered us from death. Through His resurrection has come the cry of the Faithful Believers that established the Church, gave hope for world redemption, and for the Triumph of the Son.

This is my third journey with my good friend Tim (Charles Timothy Prutzer, the master artist). I have now written three books and he has illustrated them all with splendor. What an amazing journey! His paintings express the heart-cry of my writings and I believe my writing expresses his artwork. And so it should be.

This book would not have come to be without the assistance of the Rhema Foundation. The financial underwriting of the three book projects by Rhema has made them possible.

My son Michael has grasped the soul and the spirit of these writings and has edited and formatted them in ways that excite me. There is a poetry in his spacing and positioning of words and phrases that presents the great events of history as a crescendo. Nothing is as important to me as to have Michael assist me in this project.

This is also my third journey with Toni Smith, my secretary, and Kathryn Lobley, my paralegal. Their assistance on these books has been invaluable. I thank them for their love and support for me and for my projects.

The most important person in my life is Jeanette. For more than forty years, she has tolerated my single-mindedness. God has blessed us and is still blessing us with three wonderful children, Paula, Janet and Michael, and two outstanding grandchildren, Carly and Hunter.

What an amazing life journey! And it is far from over!

Bill Hunter
Dalhart, Texas, September 2005

editor's note

When Dad first showed me his text, I was struck by the way these Biblical stories had been distilled into such concrete and imagistic poetry, drawing attention to the remarkable -- and often very visual -- structures of symbols and their repetitions that constitute the Hebrew scriptures.   In working on the textual layout of this book, I have tried to find a way to accentuate that concrete and *immediate* quality, by thinking of the blank page as a painter's canvas, and attempting to find the spirit of each section and render it in graphic form. At the same time, I have attempted to create visual repetitions throughout the book that will evoke the sense of the scriptures' own, deeply poetic, repetitions.

In the late 19th-century, a group of poets now known as the Symbolists revolutionized the way we think about poetry by considering words in their visual, and not only their auditory, aspects.   The most influential of these poets, Stéphane Mallarmé, saw the blank spaces between words on the page as positive characters, rather than just negative space.   His innovations in typography emphasized the concreteness of the words: he used blank space as a way of surrounding certain words, as if holding them up to the light for deeper scrutiny. In this way, he hoped that words might recapture some of their mystery and power (their poetry), having been rendered banal by too much everyday use. In Mallarmé's poetry, the page itself became a work of art. I am indebted to his legacy for my work on this book; and I thank my Dad for the opportunity to collaborate on such a rewarding project.

Michael Hunter
San Francisco, California, September 2005

prologue
the Father's Family

At a moment in eternity
before days began

a host of Angels appeared in Heaven

before the Father
the Son
Spirit

praising the Father
glorifying the Son
with voices
ringing

into

infinity

a hush fell on the assembly
as Father spoke

I am lonely
I want a family –
like us
blood of our blood
bone of our bone
heart of our heart
mind of our mind
spirit of our Spirit
and we will call them

Man

let them rule
    reign
    have dominion
over the place
we will create
    the place named Terra
    the place called Earth

let them share with us
    our love
    our joy
    our dreams
    our plans for Earth
        for man

let them be
our glorious example
for all creation
    of our love
    of their faithfulness
as they learn
    to trust us
    to share our love
    to do My will
and as they become
one
with you

                my Son

and one with me

let them be our family

Son spoke

        but they must learn
        these things
                Father
        and while they are learning
        they may turn away
        and if we allow man
           to rule
           to reign
           to have dominion
        over Earth
        then they must
           rule
           reign
        over Earth
        forever
        and they may take that authority
        use it to their own ends
        or give it to another

a long silence
fell on the assembly
as Father
      Son
          Spirit

           contemplated
           the creation
           of man

finally
Son spoke

                                                            Father
      when they stumble
            fall
            turn away

      when they take authority
      over Earth
      or give it to another
      I will go to them
            as the Son of Man
            as the Lamb of God
            as the King of Kings
      I will be
            their Deliverer
      I will be
            the Tree of Life
      that they may live
            in Me
            in you
                                                              Father

Father spoke

His voice
ringing
into
infinity

Son

You have the power to create

let creation commence
let days begin

let us have a family

(And it was so.)

book one

the Covenant
with Man

"A parenthesis is a phrase
or sentence inserted in another
which is grammatically complete without it,
and if you want to understand the author,
pay particular attention to the parenthesis.

God puts a parenthesis in the middle
flow of our lives - if you want to
understand your life, read the
parenthesis if you can . . . . .
(W)hen God sums up our lives, it
is the parentheses which really
give the heart of our lives with Him."

Oswald Chambers
Christian Disciplines, p.100

one
the Fall

at another moment in
eternity

the Angels of light came together in the Heavens

praising the Father
glorifying the Son

but their eyes were fixed
on a small
ball-like
object

in the midst of
celestial glory

isn't it beautiful

one Angel declared

this dream of the Father
this creation of the Son

look at the mountains
so beautiful
such a place for worship
look at the rivers
all of the fish
look at the animals

how beautiful it is
this place named Terra
this place called Earth

and as they looked
they saw Father

> walking on Earth
> searching for
> the most beautiful place

> and He came to a garden
> between four rivers
> and He stood and surveyed
> all that the Son had created
> and He smiled and said

It is good.

He loves it

> an Angel declared

it is so beautiful

> said another

the most beautiful place
on the beautiful Earth

He calls this place Eden
so like paradise
so like Heaven

but the Father is still lonely

> another declared

how can He be lonely
in such a beautiful place?

as they watched
the Father knelt to the ground
took the clay

> and in loving care
> began
> to shape it

what is he doing?
                              the Angels of light asked
                                    almost in unison

he is shaping something from the clay

look at it
how beautiful it is
it looks like the Father
it looks like the Son
the most beautiful of all creation
                                        perfect
                                        lovely
                                        like the Son

and as they watched
the Father breathed His Spirit
into this new creation
                    and it
                    began
                    to move

it is alive

                              the Angels whispered
it is like the Father
it is like the Son

                              so perfect
                              so beautiful

                        and some of the Angels
                          joyously proclaimed
so this is the dream
        of the Father
so this is the prized creation
        of the Son
no longer will the Father be lonely

for he has created

        one like Himself
        one to love
        one for fellowship

and as they watched
a deep sleep came upon
the new creation

and the Father
knelt over the new creation
        and in loving care
        took   a part
        from the side of it

what is He doing?

                one asked

He has taken one from the other
        declared another Angel
now there are two
and the second is more beautiful
than the first

look at it

            precious
            perfect
            tender

how could anything be more beautiful?

as they watched

the Father turned
to the first
and lovingly proclaimed

you are man
your name is Adam
you are a part of Me
My life is your life

He turned to the second
and said

you are woman
your name is Eve
you are a part of man
the love of his life
you are a part of Me

He spoke to both

this Earth is yours
you have dominion
I give it to you

rule
reign

forever

and the Father walked with them
and He sat with them by the river
and they walked together to the mountain tops
and He taught them things of Earth
things of Heaven
for they were friends
they fellowshipped together

and they
loved
one another.

days passed on Earth

and moments in eternity

and the Father watched His prized creations
as they cared for the garden

so perfect

an Angel proclaimed

so special to the Father
such a treasure for the Son

the Father is no longer lonely

another declared
such joyful fellowship between them

for they
are
as one.

                    at another moment in eternity
the Angels of light assembled in the Heavens

                              praising the Father
                              glorifying the Son

once again their eyes
        were fixed   on Terra
                            the place called Earth

        and Spirit
                who was one
                with the Father
                one with the Son
                        spoke to all of the Angels

        this is the day of decision
        a special day on Earth
        a day for choice

        decision
                              declared one Angel

        choice
                              proclaimed another
        how can it be?
        will the Father give man and woman
                the right to decide?
        what about Lucifer?
        what about the Angels who followed Lucifer?
        how can He give man and woman
                the right to choose?

all of the Angels of light
were silent
                    as they contemplated
                                        what was
                                        happening
                                        on the
                                        beautiful
                                        Earth

                                            finally
                                    Spirit spoke

        what is love
                        without the right not to love?
        what does it mean
        for man to be
        obedient
                        without the right to disobey?
        how can there be
        fellowship
                                without mutual trust?
        how can they be
        the Father's friends
                        unless they choose to be?

        so there must be
        a day of decision
        a time to choose
                                    and so this was
                                    the day of decision
                                    this was
                                    the time of choice

all of the Angels looked to Earth
watched the man
watched the woman
as they stood before   two

                                               trees

        look at that beautiful tree
                                an Angel whispered

        they will choose that tree
                                whispered another
        for it is the Tree of Life

                                another Angel asked
        but what if they choose the other?
                the one that gives knowledge
                reveals good
                introduces evil
        what if they choose that tree?

and while they watched

                                another Angel spoke
                                        in horror
                what is that serpent doing there
                talking to the woman?
                don't listen to him
                woman
                get her away from him
                man

then
                in silence
                        they watched
                        as
                                first
                                        the woman
                                then
                                        the man

                                        ate
                                                the fruit

                                                of that
                                                tree

                in the distance
                in another Heaven
                they could hear
                the Angels of darkness rejoicing

                                        they could hear
                                                Lucifer
                                                shout

        it's mine
        beautiful Earth
        they gave it to me

        how deceivable
                                        the woman
        how stupid
                                        the man

and a strange thing happened
on beautiful
Earth

        the beautiful man   lost part of his beauty
        the lovely woman   lost part of her loveliness
        darkness
                    death
                despair
                            descended
                                on
                                beautiful

                                        Earth

and the Garden of Eden
the most beautiful place
was closed to them
forever

how can it be?
is there no hope on Earth?
one Angel whispered

finally
Spirit spoke

this is not the end
but the beginning
the Father's plan for Earth
will be fulfilled
death on Earth
will give way to life
darkness will change
to light
despair will yield
to hope
the Father will search the Earth
for a man
to fulfill his plans

for there will always be a remnant

there will always be a man

two
the Further Fall

at another moment in eternity

the Angels of light appeared
  in the Heavens

        praising the Father
        glorifying the Son

once again
their eyes were fixed

      on Terra
      the place called Earth

isn't it lovely

       declared an Angel

but not as lovely as it was

        said another

the Father no longer
     walks
      there

       in the midst of its beauty

there is travail   where there was peace
there is darkness   where there was light
there is hate   where there was love
there is mourning where there was joy

if only they
had not eaten
of that tree

       declared another

and while they watched
        a son of Adam
        came to a place of worship

                    he
                    took
                        an animal

                                    knelt
                                    on the Earth
                                    offered it to

                                    the Father

    what is he doing?

                            one Angel asked

                            another answered
    he has taken
        that which

                                    the Father
                    gave him
                        and offered it to
                                    the Father

    a beautiful
    act of worship

                            another Angel declared

and while they watched
        a second son of Adam
        came to worship the Father

                                he offered
                            the fruit of his labors
                                the fruit of the soil

        is this his act of worship?
                                asked an Angel of light
        must he offer
        that which he produced
            the fruit of his labor?
        doesn't he realize it is an act
            of self worship?

        the Father has not
        accepted that offering
                                declared another

and as they watched
the countenance of the second son
began to change

from worship   to defiance
from reverence   to rage
from love   to hate

and he turned
to
the
first
son

and
slew
him.

and no longer was man
                    like the Father
no longer was man
                    like the Son
the mark of Cain
                was upon them
                    and rebellion
                                took over the Earth

is there no hope for Earth?
                        whispered an Angel

has Lucifer won?
                        asked another

do not forget
                            said Spirit
                there will always be a remnant

in the midst of such despair
from the loins of Adam
                            two families
                                emerged

look at the man Seth
and his family
                        declared an Angel

they are calling
upon the name of the Lord
                            said another

look at the seventh son of Seth

                              declared Spirit

the one named Enoch
he will live a full life
a year for every day
then he will be with God
a beautiful man

                         (so like the Father
                           so like the Son)

but look at the sons of men

                             said another

with the mark of Cain upon them
they worship themselves
and that which they create

                         (so like the serpent
                           so like Lucifer)

do you see the Father's plan?

                             Spirit instructed
                             the Angels

there will always be a man
with the Spirit of Enoch
            there will always be a remnant

and in the midst of darkness
that man
that remnant
will walk in light

but as time passed on Earth
the sons of God
married the daughters of men
and travail was upon the Earth

for there was no difference
between the sons of God
and the sons of men

sin and rebellion
took over Earth

and over every place
on beautiful Earth

was a shadow
of that
terrible
tree

once again
        the Angels of Heaven
        watched
        in despair

        is there no hope on Earth?
        have they all turned away?
        is there no

                        man

                                to stand
                                before the Father?

        remember

                                        said Spirit

        the Father will always have a man
                        there will always be
                        one
                        with the Spirit of Enoch

                                to stand
                                before the Father

three
the Ark Builder

with Spirit's words
        ringing in their ears
                                    the Angels of Heaven
                            looked again to Earth
                        to one solitary man named

                    Noah

            with a large piece of wood in his hands

        what is he doing?
                                    asked one Angel

        he is building something
                                answered another

and for a fleeting moment in eternity
                                        (but year
                                        after year
                                        on Earth)
                they watched the labor
                of that solitary man
                turn into
                        a magnificent structure

        it's so large
        what is it?
        what is he doing?
                                    an Angel asked

        it's an ark
        a place of refuge
                        another joyously responded

and as they watched
     a strange thing began to occur on Terra

          as animals came from near
          and animals came from far
               two by two
                they came
        from all over the Earth

     something is going to happen
     on Earth
               declared an Angel
    the waters will be a place of death
    that ark will be a place of life

the Father placed that man
              his family
           those animals
            two by two

      in that ark

                  and He
                  closed
                  them
                  in

      and water came from the deep
      and water came from above
      and the water on Earth was
           the water of death
      but to those in the ark it was
            water of life

that solitary man

                                        his family
                                 those animals
                                  two by two
                 were carried forth
                    in that ark

                                              to a
                                              place
                                              of dry
                                              ground

           and a radiant rainbow
           reached from Heaven to Earth
           a sign of new hope
           and promise

                                        and the voices
                              of a chorus of Angels
                                rang from the Heavens
                 there will always be a man
                 there will always be an ark
                 there will always be a rainbow

                                 from the other Heaven
                                   came a defiant cry
                 but most will follow Lucifer

                                       and a response
                             from the Angels of God
                 but some will follow the Father
                 some will always rest in the ark

                       for there will always be a remnant

and from the Heaven of Heavens

the Father spoke
to that man

I have watched you

Noah

as you faithfully built that ark
as a place of refuge
for your family

but your family
will not be faithful
as you were faithful

Noah

and they will scatter

over all of Earth

most will not follow you
most will turn from Me
but some will follow
for there will always be a remnant
and for that remnant
a rainbow will appear
to remind them
of your faithfulness

Noah

and my love for you
and my love for your family

And it was so.

four
the Promisekeeper

once again
      darkness
      was upon the Earth
                  as if all had turned from the Father

                  and the same words
                          rang
                  from the Heavens
   is there no hope on Earth?

      as the Angels looked
      at the darkness
      on Earth
                  they heard
            the Father speak

My Son
My Spirit
it is time for Our Family

      as the Father spoke these words
      the eyes of the Angels were riveted
      on one man
            at a place called Ur
            packing his possessions
            preparing for a journey

this is the Father's man

                Spirit said

his loins will produce the remnant
he will be the Father's man
man of faith

where does he plan to go?

                      an Angel asked

he does not know

                      answered another
he is going
because the Father has called him
and he will go
wherever the Father asks him to go

      and they watched that man
      travel to a new land
        a land the Father gave him

isn't this land beautiful

                    declared an angel
the place the Father led him

           a
           most
           beautiful place
           on Earth

but it's not like the Garden

                    another proclaimed
and the beautiful tree
is not there

as they watched
they could hear

                   the words of the Father
                    spoken to that man
you have followed Me
     to a place you didn't know
you have trusted Me
     you are my friend
your name is

          Abraham

in your old age
I will give to you
the son of the Promise
your seeds will be as the sand
your seeds will be as the stars
you will produce
     children of your loins
     children of your spirit

               And it was so.

on another day

             the Angels assembled
                 and in quiet contemplation
                 they watched from Heaven

     as this man

           Abraham

             and his son
             his only
             son
                 began
                 to climb
                 a mountain

     what are they doing?
             one asked

     they are going up to worship
             another answered

as the man

          and his
          son
                 reached the
                 top
                 of the
                 mountain

       there was an

          altar

          ready
             (for sacrifice)

they are ready to worship
where is the sacrifice?
where is
the lamb?

                                    an Angel asked

                              another quietly replied
the Father will provide the sacrifice
the Father will provide
the lamb

but they watched   (in amazement)
                        as
                        the man's son
                        his only son
                                    climbed
                                    onto that
                                    altar

        and the man stood over him
        with a knife in his hand
        preparing to offer the son
        to the Father in love
        and the Angels
        couldn't believe
        what was happening
        and all they could say was

how can this be?

                                        and then
                                          words
                                           came

                                  from the Father
                                        of Heaven

it is enough
it is finished
you love Me
you trust Me
you are my friend
spare
                        your son
                        your only son
I will provide
the lamb

                   and there
                   in a thicket
                   was a ram

            a lamb from the Father
            a lamb for the altar
            a lamb for the sacrifice

                                     the Angels
                                      joyously
                                    proclaimed
we know why
the Father created them
such love of the Father
such love of the man
such a union between them
a binding together
as friends

and Heaven rang
with the voices
of Angels
praising the Father
glorifying the Son

and as they looked again to Terra

to the man
and his son
embracing
on that mountain

behind the lamb
behind the altar
they saw a shadow
of a cross
and a giant shadow
of that beautiful tree

as
Abraham
and his son
walked
down
from that mountain

the Father's words
spoken from Heaven
softly echoed
in Abraham's heart

49

Abraham

you trusted me
like no other man
you followed me
rested in my promise
I love you
and from your loin
I will produce
a beautiful tree

but those of your seed
who do not trust me
as you trusted me
will be torn from that tree

but those of the seed
of your spirit
who do trust me
will be grafted to the tree

that tree will be
the tree of promise
like the beautiful tree
that grew in Eden

And it was so.

                                    and a chorus erupted
                                            in Heaven

there will always be a man
there will always be a remnant
there will always be an ark
there will always be a sacrifice

     there will always be

                                        that
                                   beautiful
                                        tree

five
the Deliverer

                    at another moment in eternity

          after decades on Earth
          passed
          from one century to another

the Angels of Heaven
once again
fixed their eyes
                         on Earth

                    at a place called
                              Egypt

          they are all here
                              one Angel whispered
          all in Egypt
          the seeds of Abraham's loins
          they are all slaves of Pharaoh

                              another Angel replied
          how can it be?
          there was such promise

and to add to their despair they heard from
                    Egypt
          the decree of Pharaoh that all newborn sons of
                         Abraham
                              must die in the river Nile

but as they watched

the light of Heaven
began to shine

on a mother

with tears in her eyes
but hope in her heart

who placed a little child
in a small ark

and pushed the ark
in the river of death

and by a providential act

(that only God can do)

that little ark
with the small child

passed through the river of death
to the loving arms
of the daughter of Pharaoh

and Pharaoh's daughter
called the mother of the child
to care for the child
in Pharaoh's house

and the Angels of light
rejoiced

so this is the plan of the Father
this is the victory of the Son
God has provided a child
God has provided an ark
God has provided a deliverer
and God will provide a remnant

forty years passed to eighty

                    and that little child
                    now a broken man
                    walked alone
                    on the back side
                    of the desert

      he doesn't look like a deliverer
                    an Angel proclaimed
      he's a broken man
      at the back side
      of the desert
      he has gone
      as far
      as he can go

but while they watched
                a small bush
                    burst
                into flames

                            (and would not
                              stop burning)

and from His throne in Heaven
came the marvelous words
of the Father of love

spoken to
that broken man
at the back side
of the desert
Moses

take off your shoes
you stand where I have placed you
on Holy Ground
you are my deliverer
of my enslaved people

and a weak response
came
from that broken man
Father

I am nothing
I can not go
see how weak I am
I'm afraid of Pharaoh
I can't stand up to him

I even
stutter

but if you tell me to go

I will go

                              and from the throne
                                        in Heaven
                            came these loving words

                    Moses

you passed through the water by my hand
you traveled the way I led you
your days in the desert
prepared you for my calling
your weakness
has made you humble
your failures
have caused you to trust me
go back
                    Moses

deliver my people
                                        from the hand
                                          of Pharaoh

                    Moses

          turned
          toward Egypt
          his face set like flint
          an obedient servant
          eyes fixed
          on Pharaoh's house

                    and almost in a blink
                              of their eyes
                        the Angels watched
                        a struggle on Earth
                    like they had never seen

as the Father of Heaven
through his servant

            Moses

        fought against Lucifer
        for the deliverance from Pharaoh
        of the children of Abraham

          in
          rapid
          succession
          three plagues erupted
          throughout all of Egypt

          first
        blood on the water
            then
        frogs everywhere
            then
        gnats from the ground

                and the joyous cry
            came from the other Heaven
             from the mouth of Lucifer

they are all mine
even Abraham's children
see what is happening
they have all sinned
the blood of their sins is on the water
they are all proud and arrogant
                like the frog
the curse of the Father
          like gnats from the ground
torments them

                              and from the Father's
                                      Heaven
                      the Angels of light whispered

        how can it be?
        Abraham's children
        trapped by their sins
        self-sufficient
        rebellious
        under the curse of the Father
        is there no hope?

while they pondered
the three plagues

                        three more plagues erupted
                        in
                        rapid
                        succession
                        in Pharaoh's land

                        first
                flies covered the people of Egypt
                        then
                the livestock died
                        then
                Moses cast ashes in the air

                and boils erupted
                on every living thing
                where the ashes fell

                                        and the cry of Lucifer
                                                  louder
I am Beelzebub
lord of the flies
they are mine
I have dominion over them
the Father will not accept
            their livestock
                    the fruit of
                    their self-made labors
the Father will not accept
            their worship

                                        his rejoicing
                                        changed to rage
                                                shouting
what is happening?
those plagues
did not touch
Abraham's children

                                        in defiance
                                        shouting
                            at the Father of Heaven
what have you done?
they are mine
you can't win
I won't let them go

                                        with a voice
                            ringing throughout Egypt
                                Lucifer shouting
                                        even louder
don't let them go Pharaoh
they belong to you
they belong to me
don't let them go

and while Lucifer shouted

        three more plagues erupted
        in Egypt

    first hail
        judgment from Heaven
        battering Pharaoh's land
   then
   locusts
        devouring everything
        the hail did not destroy
   then
   darkness
        covering all Egypt
        so dark none could see

                (even Pharaoh
                    fell
                in the dark)

but light shone brightly
on the children of Abraham

    Pharaoh don't give in to Him
                Lucifer shouted
            from the other Heaven
    they are yours
    they are mine
    don't let them go

when Lucifer stopped shouting
    a strange thing happened
        in the land of
            Abraham's children

                each father took a lamb
                slew the lamb
                looked to Heaven
                placed the blood of the lamb
                on the door of his house

and from Heaven came a devourer to the land of Egypt
to destroy the first born son in each house
where there was no blood
of the lamb

        the sound of crying rang from all of Egypt
        as death took the oldest son of each Egyptian home

           but in the land of
           Abraham's children
           there was peace

                        (not even a dog
                            wagged
                              its tongue)

           over each house
           marked by the blood
           a shadow of a cross
           with the form of a man
           hanging upon that cross
           and a giant shadow
           of that beautiful tree

                    and from the other Heaven
                            the cry of Lucifer
Pharaoh don't let them go
they belong to me
they are my slaves

                    the words of Lucifer
                    rang in the mind
                    of Pharaoh

                    in his heart

                            and Pharaoh cried out
                                    defiantly
don't let them go
they belong to me
they are my slaves

                    in their despair
                            death
                    darkness
                                    the voices of
                    commanders of thousands
                            captains of hundreds
                                    leaders of tens
                                    began to ring
                            throughout Egypt
prepare to march after them
they belong to Pharaoh
don't let them go

the Angels of Heaven
　　　　watched the joyous journey
　　　　　　　of Abraham's children
　　　　　　　　　　traveling from Egypt
　　　　　　　　　　　　under the light of the Son

　　　　　　　　　　　　　and behind them
　　　　　　　　　　stumbling in darkness
　　　　　　　　traveling in despair
　　　　　　came the army of Pharaoh
　　　　seeking to return them as slaves

as Moses led them
　　　　they came to a sea　　　　too deep to cross
　　　　　　　and all of Abraham's children
　　　　　　　　　　　looked at the water
　　　looked at Pharaoh's army
　　　　　　　and turned to Moses
　　　　　　　　　　　　　　crying

　　　　you are no deliverer
　　　　you led us to our death
　　　　how happy we were in Egypt

　　　　　　　Moses
　　　　　　　lifted his eyes
　　　　　　　to Heaven
　　　　　　　　　　spoke to the Father
　　　　　　　　　as a man speaks to a friend
Father
separate the water
let it be the water of life　　　　to Abraham's children
let it be the water of death　　　　to Pharaoh's army

　　　　　　　　　And it was so.

66

and

                              Moses

and

                    Abraham's children

                                      no longer slaves
                                      now the children
                                    of the Father

passed through the water
on dry ground
                    this same water
                    water of death
                    to Pharaoh's army
                                            buried
                                  in the bottom
                                      of the sea

as days passed on Earth

                        Moses

        led

                        the people of the Father

the children of Abraham

  through the great wilderness

          when they were thirsty

          the Father gave them

          water from the rock

            when they were hungry

            food came from Heaven

            to satisfy their hunger

                        Spirit

           was a cloud over them

        to protect them from the heat

       when they were cold

       in the middle of the night

                  the Son

             was a light

          to keep them warm

          none of Egypt's diseases

          touched Abraham's children

          their clothes

          did not wear out

they were

Abraham's children

the children of the promise

                no longer slaves

                now children

                of the Living God

                              but from Abraham's children
                                              came a cry
                                                    defiant
          we don't like it out here
          it is not like Egypt
          we were happy there
          why did you bring us
          to this wilderness to die?

                                      and the Angels asked
          how can they turn
          so quickly
          from the Father?
          do they not understand
          that they were slaves
          and now they are free
          because Moses delivered them?
          will they always be slaves
          in their hearts
          in their minds?
          do they love Lucifer
          more than the Father?

while they watched
                              Moses

                                        led
                                        the people
                                        to a great mountain

                              Moses

                                        and his servant Joshua
                                        went up that mountain
                                        to talk to the Father

Abraham's children
stood in fear
as that mountain shook
under the power of the Father

                              the Father
                        spoke to Moses
                  on top of that mountain

                                a voice
                          that the people
                        heard as thunder
                                 Moses
                                 heard
                          as words of life

            Moses

      you have been my faithful deliverer
      you have obeyed me like no other man
      now you will be my lawgiver
      you will proclaim my law
      you will be my prophet
                        so like my Son
                        who will be
                        my Great Prophet
      some will listen to you
      but most will not
      for some trust me
      as Abraham trusted me
                  for there will always be a remnant
      but most of them are hard of heart
                              rebellious
                              stubborn
      faithfully tell them my words

my words are life
to those who obey
but my words are death
to those who do not
just as the water was life
to those who trusted me
and death to those
who did not

                                    finally Moses spoke

I want to know you Father
I want to see you Father
if I must lead them
if I must teach them
show me your glory

                                    and the Father
                                    answered Moses

I cannot walk with you
              as a friend
              as I walked
          with my friend
                Adam
because you would not live
              since Eve
          and her husband
                Adam
              ate of that tree
but I will hide you in the rock
for my Son is that Rock
and you can see my back
as I pass by

                                  And it was so.

as
　　Moses

　　　spent days
　　　on the mountain
　　　listening to the Father
　　　　the Father told Moses
　　　　wonderful things
　　　　of Heaven
　　　　of Earth
　　　　　of the Father
　　things that Moses
　　was to proclaim
　to Abraham's children

　　　　　　finally the Father said
go down
　　　Moses
go down from the mountain
lead your people
they have all turned away
worshiping gods
that they made
with their own hands
lead them
　　　Moses
　　　　　to the land
　　　　　I gave to Abraham

　　build me a tabernacle
　　and I will travel with them
　　they cannot come near me
　　because of their rebellion
　　because of that tree
　　but you may come near me

I will lead you
and you can lead them

give them my laws
            Moses
tell them about me

              most will not listen
              but some will listen

      for there will always be a remnant

and at the end of your journey
            Moses
your servant Joshua
and my warrior Caleb
will lead them
                  to the land
            I gave to Abraham
but none of this generation
                  save Joshua
                  and Caleb
will enter Abraham's land
they have refused to accept my provision
   they have murmured and complained
            they do not trust me
            they will not obey me
            therefore

              they may not enter
            into Abraham's land

              And it was so.

six
the Lionkiller

once again
the Angels of light
looked to Earth
to Abraham's land
the place the Father
gave
to
Abraham
and his children

they are here now
in Abraham's land
they have completed their journey
said an Angel
but   Joshua
(Moses' servant)
and   Caleb
(the warrior)   are both dead
and   Abraham's children
are not   one
but   twelve
divided into separate
tribes
said another Angel
and each tribe
is under   its own standard
and there is no
unity   between
them
and there is no one to lead   them
for they have   turned
from the Father
said another

as moments passed in eternity
         the Angels watched
                  as one judge
                  then another
                                    was raised by the Father
                                             to lead his tribe
                  and then
                  there were no
                  more judges
                  and every man
                  did what was
                  right
                  in his own eyes
         and a shadow
                           of that terrible tree
                  was over all of
              Abraham's land
and from Earth
         came
                                             the desperate cry
                           of Abraham's children
                           first in a few whispers
                                    then in a loud roar
         we have no leader
         we have no king
         give us a king
         like the other nations have
                                    and the Angels
                                       whispered
                                       in unbelief
         they have rejected the Father
         they have rejected the Son
         how can they ask
                  for another to rule them?

while they watched
                a man
                named
                Saul
                was chosen
                                as their king

        he looks like a king
                                                said an Angel

        tall
        strong

        but the Father
        looks at the heart
        and not the body
                                                said another

while they watched
                that   King
                that first King of Israel
                that   King of Abraham's children

                                quickly turned
                                from the Father

                        refusing
                                        to do
                                        His will
                        seeking
                                        the praise
                                        of men
                        and not
                                        the praise
                                        of the Father

immediately

the words
of the Father

through
his servant
Samuel

were spoken
to

that
King

the Father named you King
but you have disobeyed Him
now the kingdom
is torn from you
and given to another

as moments passed

      the Angels of Heaven
      again looked to Earth
         to a quiet valley
        and a   boy
            watching some sheep

      that boy is
            David
      a descendant of Judah
                said Spirit
      he is God's chosen king

      but he is so small
              said an Angel
      he doesn't look
      like a King

as they watched
      a lion approached the sheep
      ready to attack them
         and   David
                   cried
                at the top
              of his voice

      the Father
      is my strength
      and my salvation

and he grabbed the lion

                     and
                   killed
                   it.

and from Heaven

the voice of the Father
rang in that valley

David

you love me
you trust me
I will call you

lionkiller

for you are my little

lion

of the tribe of Judah

after the passing of
a moment in eternity
the Angels watched that same boy

with a slingshot
and five small rocks
in
his hand

stand before
a giant man
named Goliath
boldly proclaiming

the Father named me

lionkiller

I have killed the lion
I have killed the bear
if the Father gave me strength
to slay the lion
and the bear
He will deliver you

Goliath

into my hands

and the small   boy
                    cast
                    the   first
                                 stone
                    at
                                 the giant's
                                 head

                                              and
                                              slew
                                              him.

                                        the voice of the Father
                                        came from Heaven
                                            to that small boy

          you are only a boy

                            David

          and your body is small
              but your heart is big
          and I look at your heart
              and not your body
          and when I look at your heart
          I see the heart of a lion
                                        so like my Son
                                        who will be
                                        the lion
                                        of the tribe of Judah

          and I have chosen you as my King

   as the Angels watched from Heaven
   and as days passed on Earth
                            this little David

                                        now a man
                            with a heart like the Father's heart
                                            started his journey
                                            to his throne

                    as King of Israel

   but his journey began
   not at the throne
   crown on his head
   but riding a donkey
   fleeing from
                                        King Saul

and he drew to him
        as his followers
        those who were
                in distress
                discontent
                hopeless
                        and they became
                        his mighty men
                                for they would
                                follow him
                                        even to the end

and when
                                                Saul
drew near
                                some of
                                David's
                                mighty men
                                        cried out

kill him
kill him
                                but David
                                lionkiller
                                        stern
                                        replied

get thee behind me
                        Lucifer
I will not raise my hand
        against the Lord's anointed
I will be the king
        when the Father calls me
I will not now
        test the Father
by raising my hand
        against His anointed one

as the Angels watched

                        David

                             the little
                             lionkiller
                                   the Father's
                                   chosen king

          travel through Abraham's land
                        they heard his words
                  ringing through the Heavens
the Lord is my rock
      my fortress and my deliverer
my God is my rock in whom I take refuge
He is my shield
      the horn of my salvation
      my stronghold
He reached down from on high and took hold of me
He drew me out of deep waters
He rescued me from my powerful enemy
He makes my feet like the feet of a deer
He enables me to stand on the heights
He trains my hands for battle
      my arms can bend a bow of bronze
You give me your shield of victory
      and your right hand sustains me
You have delivered me from the attacks of the people
You have made me the head of nations
                    The Lord lives!
                    Praise be to my Rock!
                    Exalted be God my Savior!

while the Angels watched
      with tears in their eyes
                    one of them whispered
                        quietly
      now I know why the Father loves him so much

on the day of

                                        Saul's
                                      death
                         the Father's words
                     spoken from Heaven
                                rang
             throughout Abraham's land

my little lionkiller

today I have installed
you as king
in Jerusalem
        my chosen city
today I have begotten you
ask of me and I will give you
Jerusalem
        as your inheritance
and Abraham's land
and all of the land
I promised to
        Abraham
        Isaac
        Jacob

                  and David
                  became
                  the Father's beloved king
                          so like the Son
                          who would be
                     the King of Kings

days passed
          the Angels of Heaven
          watched that same
                        David
          as King of Israel

                              standing in his house
                              watching a beautiful
                  woman
     as she unclothed
     to bathe

                              one Angel whispered
          what is he doing
          looking at that woman?
                        another proclaimed
          why is that serpent
          talking to him?
                                   another
                                   in horror
                                   proclaimed
          don't listen to that serpent
                        David
          don't look at that woman

as the Angels watched
                        the   serpent
                                   softly
                                   spoke
                                   to David

     isn't she beautiful?
     you are king
     you have dominion

why don't you
take
her?

and   King David
                                   King of Israel

took
that
woman
                        into his house
                        into his bed
and then he got up from his bed

                                        and
                                        slew
                                        her
                                        husband.

and a strange thing happened in Israel

                darkness
                despair
                division
                      descended
                          upon the
                              House
                              of David

and an older son of David forced a daughter of David to his
bed and when the older son got up from that bed
a second son of David

                                    slew
                                    him.

and that second son proclaimed himself as king
and King David left his palace and was forced to flee
                    from the
                    second son

                      and over the House of David
                      and over all of Israel

                            stood a giant shadow
                            of that
                            terrible tree

and from the Kingdom of Israel
     in the midst of despair
         and darkness

                                came the cry
                of
                David

                first in a faint whisper
                  then in a loud voice
   against you Father
   have I sinned

      done these terrible things

   please
   forgive me
   wash me with hyssop

   I shall be clean

                                        from Heaven
                                                 came
                                words of the Father
                                              spoken

                        to
                        David
little lionkiller
your body is weak
now you are a

                                                man killer.

but you love me like no other man
your heart is the heart of a lion
you will be my example for others
        whose bodies are weak
that I look at their hearts
        and not their bodies

nevertheless

your sins have lifted the covering from your family
you have delivered them
                                to Lucifer

because of your sins
your kingdom will be divided

and once again

                                        a cry came
                                        from the
                                Angels of Heaven

            is there no hope on Earth?

                                        but Spirit
                                        spoke
                                to the Angels

            this is not the end
            but a new beginning
            the Father's plans on Earth
            will be fulfilled
            death on Earth   will give way to life
            darkness   will change to light
            despair   will yield to hope
            and one will come
            a man from the Father
            to fulfill the Father's plans

            but before that man comes

                        David

                    will reclaim
                    his kingdom
                    from his son

                        but
                            the House of David

                    will
                        divide

through the Father's mercy
                    love
                    forgiveness
a son of that woman will be the next king
and the kingdom of that son will be a great kingdom
and after that son's death
the kingdom will divide
                        because of the sins of
                            David

many kings will rule over Israel
and some of those kings
will call upon the name of the Lord
                    with the Heart of
                        David

                                        from the other
                                            Heaven
                                        came a cry
                                            defiant
but most will follow Lucifer

                                        and a response
                                            from the
                                        Angels of God
but some will follow the Father

            for there will always be a remnant

as moments passed in eternity
                                    and days on Earth
                the Angels of Heaven
                quietly contemplated
                all that had occurred
                                on Terra
                the place called Earth

after long moments of silence
                                        one of them asked
            will man always go his own way?
            will he give the Earth over to Lucifer?

                                        the Son
                                        whispered
                                        quietly
                                    to the Father
                        (but with a voice that
                    rang through the Heavens)
                    Father
        in your time
        I will go
                        first as a child
                                    as Moses was a child
                        then as a boy
                                    so like the boy David
                        then as a man
                        who trusts You
                as Your friend Abraham trusted You
                and then as a deliverer
                            so like the deliverer Moses
            I will be the man

then the voice
of Spirit
came from the Heavens

(moved
as a quiet breeze
upon Earth)

and when the Son returns to You

Father

after He has fulfilled His mission

I will stay with them

although most will not follow the Son
some will follow

for there will be a remnant

and I will be with that remnant

I will walk with them
I will teach them things of Earth
I will teach them things of Heaven
I will be their comforter
I will reveal the Son to them
I will tell them of You

Father

and they will be Your friends

Father

and they will fellowship together
and they will love each other
and they will fellowship with Us
and they will love Us

for they will be
Our Family

the words
of the Father
came from the Heavens
echoed throughout Earth

it is
good

let it
be

And it was so.

book two

the Covenant
with the Son

I have installed My King on Zion,
My holy hill...
You are my Son;
today I have become your Father.
Ask of Me, and I will make
the nations your inheritance,
the ends of the Earth your possession...
Kiss the Son, lest He be angry
and you be destroyed in your way...
Blessed are all who take refuge in Him.

Psalms 2 (NIV)

the Triumph
of the Son of Man

At another moment
                    in eternity
the Angels of Light
appeared in the Heavens
praising the Father
and glorifying the Son

and once again
their eyes were fixed
on the place named Terra
        the place called Earth

                        it is so dark down there
said an Angel

                            there is such despair
                    and death is everywhere

                    and over the entire Earth
                        is a giant shadow
                        of that terrible tree
added another Angel

                        but the darkest place
                        is Abraham's land
said another

                            only part of
                    Abraham's children
                            live in
                    Abraham's land

                    the rest are scattered
            throughout
the
        whole
                Earth

                              and those in Abraham's land
                        do not even know
                                        where the other
                              children are
                                    and the ruler of Rome
                        is king of Abraham's land
                                    and Abraham's children
                        are his slaves
                                        how can it be?

and while they watched
they saw Abraham's children under their own standards
preparing to war against the Romans

                                        that is all they know
                              those children of Abraham
            declared an Angel
                              they only know how to fight
                              they do not trust the Father
                              and each family marches
                              under its own standard

and their eyes fixed on the standard of the leader of them
and it bore the name of the Maccabees

their religious leaders
and Abraham's
children
come near the Father
with their mouths
and honor Him
with their lips
and worship Him
in their own traditions
but their hearts
are far from Him

lamented another Angel

they do not even
realize
that they are slaves

look at what man
has produced
darkness
despair
hopelessness
violence
rage
against each other
no trust of the Father
no love among them

they do not have a King

said another

but the despair of the Angels
    changed to
    excitement
    anticipation

        as Spirit spoke

                        the Son is prepared
                                to go
                            down
                            there

                        He has told the Father
                            He will go
                        to do the Father's will
                            He will be
                        Great High Priest
                        over all of the Earth
        as Abraham
        was priest
        over his house

        an Angel added

                        and He will be Deliverer
                                and Prophet
                                for all people
                        as Moses
                        was deliverer
                        and prophet
                        for Abraham's children

                    first He must come as a child
                    then He must die as a lamb
                    then He will be
                    that beautiful tree
        added another

and in the midst of darkness
in Abraham's land
                    a light
                began to shine
                            first from Heaven to Earth
                        and then from Earth to Heaven
                on a man
            on a difficult journey
        leading a donkey
            with a woman
                with child
                    riding   on the donkey

and all of the Angels of Heaven burst into songs of praise
glorifying the Father and praising the Son
                                there He is!

                        in His mother's womb
                        Son of God
                        Son of Man
                        beginning His journey

                            He will be
                        devoted to man
                    and their salvation
                until all of the Kingdoms
                        of this Earth
                    become the Kingdom
                        of the Son

                and He will reign
                    forever
                    and
                    forever

and while the Angels sang their songs of praise
in the Heavens

      the voice of the woman riding on that donkey
      was heard quietly on the Earth
      but ringing in the Heavens
                my soul does magnify the Lord
                and my spirit does rejoice
                in God my Father
                for He has chosen me
                a humble maid-servant
                to be the mother
                of His glorious Son

      and the words of the man leading that donkey
      on the difficult journey
      also rang in the Heavens
                I do not understand
                your ways
                Father
                but I will be
                a father to your Son
                and a faithful husband
                to His mother
                 Mary

days passed

and they finished their journey and arrived
at a little town in Abraham's land
named Bethlehem
a faithful man
and a woman with child
preparing for the birth
of the King of Kings

and their journey ended
not at a palace prepared for a King
but at a stable reserved for a servant

and the King of Kings
                    the Deliverer
          the Savior
          of the whole Earth

                                   the Son of God
                    the Son of Man
                                        came to Earth
                                   as a small child

                                        born

                              in a manger

and on the day of His birth all Heaven rang
                                    with shouts of Angels

          the sun
          the moon
          all of the stars
                    were brighter
                    than they had ever been

          darkness on Earth gave way to a radiant light
          shining from the crib of that little child

     and a chorus of Angels
     resounded through the Heavens

                              this is the day of days
                                    all days past
                    have waited for this moment
                              all days to come
                         will reverence this day
                              for the Son of God
                              has this day become
                                 the Son of Man

               and He will reign
                    forever
                    and
                    forever

                                    isn't He beautiful
     whispered an Angel

                              so like Adam
                              before he ate
                         of that terrible tree

as days passed

                  this
                  little
                  child
                      walked with His father
                          Joseph

and His father taught Him the trade of a carpenter
and He sat at His mother's feet as she taught Him
                          things of Heaven
                          things of the Earth

        but His most joyous days
        were spent on the mountain
        with the Father
        and the Spirit
        together as friends
                He sat with them
                  on the mountain top
                He walked with them
                  in the valley
                they talked to Him
                  of things of Heaven
                and things of Earth
                they were friends
                  they were as one
                  they loved each other

and He walked on the Earth and observed its beauty
and He went to the temple and talked to the wise
and confounded them with His wisdom

                                        this
                                        little
                                        boy

        grew

                        in wisdom

                        in stature

                        in favor
                        with God
                        and Man

on another occasion the Angels of Heaven looked to Earth
                                    to Abraham's land
          and one of them said

                              He is thirty years old
                                              now
                                    He is a man

                                    His mission
                                      is to begin
          added another

and as they watched
                         Son of God
                         Son of Man
                           was led by Spirit
                             into a desert

                           where He stayed for forty days
                           without food
                           and then He was hungry

                           this is the day of decision
                             a special day on Earth
                               a day for choice
                                 so like the day
                             when Adam and Eve
                               made their choice
          said a wise Angel

and all of the Angels of Light were
                                    (silent)
as they contemplated
what was happening in Abraham's land

and in that desert behind the Son appeared that serpent
and standing in front of the Son was the Tree of Life
and beside it was that other tree
              for this was the day of choice
              this was the time of decision

      and Lucifer appeared
      at His side
      saying to the Son

                    You are hungry
                You have the authority
                    of the Father
                  change this stone
                    to bread

      and the Son
      replied to Lucifer

                    My food
                is the Father's will
                  I will feed
                on every word
                from the mouth
                of My Father

      Lucifer led Him
      to the top of the temple
      and said to Him

              throw yourself down
              that the Angels may
                catch You
              You will prove
         that You trust the Father
         and all men will see
              Your power
              and authority

the Son replied

                              I will come
                in the name of the Father
                     and in His power
                      and authority
                        but only
                as the Father leads me
                   and I will not now
                            test
                        the Father

Lucifer continued

                       this Earth is mine
                     Adam gave it to me
                       I am the prince
                     of the whole Earth
                         worship me
                      like the others do
                      and I will give
                         all to You

the Son replied

                      only the Father
                       do I worship
                          away
                        from Me
                         Lucifer

when the Son spoke these words the serpent disappeared
and the terrible tree vanished
and Lucifer withdrew for a moment

Angels appeared from Heaven to care for the Son of Man
and while the Angels cared for Him
        the Son spoke to the Father in Heaven
                                        Father

                                I came to the Earth
                                  as Your child
                                    and now I am
                                      a man
                                      because I am
                                      Your Son
                                      I will be
                                    as no other man
                                      for I will always
                                          do Your will
                                          I will fulfill
                                          every jot
                                        every tittle
                                      of Your words
                            and when I return to You
                                none of Your words
                                    will be unfulfilled

                                          no one
                                        before Me
                                    was ever righteous
                                      but I will be
                                        righteous
                                          Father
                            and they can live
                            in My righteousness

and I will trust You Father
like Abraham trusted you
but more than Abraham
Father
for I am one with You
and You are one with me
and when their
bodies are weak
and they have no faith
they can live
in My faith

and when You call Me
as the lamb
to hang on that tree
I will be

the crucified
Lamb
of God
to take away their sins

the day of decision ended
the time of choice was over

the Son of God
the Son of Man
        set His face like flint to do the Father's will

He was different than any other man
He came as the Word
        the Word made flesh to dwell among them

those who followed Him beheld His glory
the glory of the Father manifested on Earth

His words were for the healing of the nations
He was the light of the world
        to show the way

to those who received Him
who called upon His name
        He gave them power
        to become the children of the Living God

for three years   He walked among them
for three years   He told them about His Father
                         He taught them things of Heaven
                                 and things of Earth
                         He was their friend
                         He loved them more than life itself

                         He drew to Him
                                 twelve
                                    who would follow Him
                                 eleven
                                    at the moment
                                 and
                                 one
                                               out of season
they were His special companions
                         He called them His disciples

                         He told them of the Father's love
                                 for the Son
                                 and for them
                         He loved the Father
                            more than anything else
                         He wanted them to know
                                         love
                                         respect
                                         obey
                                     His Father
                                     as much as He

He drew to Him
those who were
in distress
sick
discontent
sinful
without hope

those
rejected by men

and
like He
men of sorrow
acquainted with grief

He looked at their hearts
and not their bodies
He drew to Him
those who would follow Him
even to the end

and most did not follow Him
for they loved darkness more than light
and they loved their traditions more than the Living Word
to them there was no beauty about Him
nothing in His appearance to attract them to Him

and they rejected Him

they despised Him
reviled Him

when they looked upon Him
they did not see
                the Son of God
                the Son of Man
but a man of sorrow
        from whom
        they hid their faces

but to all who would listen
he spoke words   of life
              of healing
                    of love
                  of salvation
        of forgiveness
               of truth
                  of hope

                (if all of His words
                  were recorded
    even Heaven could not contain them)

as His days on Earth drew near to a close

      Spirit spoke softly
      to the Angels of light
                    His days with them
                      were so few
                 and He traveled
           such a short distance
             most men on Earth
        do not know of His coming

           but this Solitary Man
              will transform
            the whole Earth
     from the Kingdom of Lucifer
            to the Kingdom
           of the Son of God
    and He will reign
      forever
      and
      forever

at the end of those three years
Son of God
Son of Man
      completed His journey throughout Abraham's land
      He did everything that the Father asked Him to do
      not one thing the Father told Him
      remained unfulfilled

and then
this Solitary Man

destined to change
the whole Earth

this Son of God
this Son of Man
this Lamb for the slaughter

set His face

like flint

with His eyes fixed

on a hill called

      Golgotha

           (place
           of the
           skull)

two
Triumph
of the Crucified

at
another
moment
in eternity

      the Angels of Light
      looked again to Earth
      and to Abraham's land

                  there He is

whispered an Angel

          entering Jerusalem
          riding on a donkey
          so like the day
          He entered Bethlehem
          riding on a donkey
          in His mother's womb

          but few noticed
          in that day of His coming

said another

          and now
          all
          are watching Him

as they watched

    Abraham's children

             spread palm branches
                before Him

    and shouted
    almost in unison

             Hosanna Hosanna
             blessed is He
             who comes
        in the name of the Lord

             such love of Him

    said an angel

             such worship
             and reverence

             but they will soon
             turn against Him

    added Spirit

as they watched

       this
       solitary
       man

           Son of God
           Son of Man

     concluded
     His journey

           not at a palace
           to be proclaimed their king

    not at the temple
    as their priest

        but in an upper room
        alone with His disciples
        as their servant

He shared with them His last supper
He told them things of Heaven and of Earth
He told them of His Father

        as a loving child
        proud of His Father
        He shared with them
        the Father of Love

He told them of His destiny
in words they did not understand

           I must go away
           for if I do not go
             Spirit
           will not come
       and Spirit must come

           to lead you
           comfort you
           teach you of Me
        teach you of the Father

He told them words of eternal life

I am the vine
you are the branches
as the branches
you are one with Me
and one with the Father
and you will live
with Us forever

He prayed for Himself

Father
the time has come
for sacrifice
I have brought You glory
now glorify Me
in Your presence
with the glory
that I had
before I became
the Son of Man

He prayed for His disciples

Father
I have revealed
You to them
they are Yours
they are Mine
because You gave
them to Me
I have taught them
Your words
I have cared for them
I have protected them
these eleven
my disciples

and I will care
for
the twelfth
the one born
out of season
none will be lost
now I will return to You
protect them
care for them
sanctify them
establish them in truth
for I have given My life
for them
and for all others
who will
believe

and He prayed for all
who will believe in Him

Father
may they all be one
as We are one
one with Me
one with You
one with each other
I want them
to see My glory
the glory You gave Me

through them
Father
may the world believe
that You sent Me

but the prayer that caused the Angels

         to cry

  was the agonizing prayer
    of the Son
    as He sweat

        drops

          of blood

   prayed at

     Gethsemene

    to His Father in Heaven

        Father

     if there is some other way
      for their salvation
    for their righteousness
     for the removal
      of their sins

      may it be

     if that will not be
      let Me drink
      of the cup
     You prepared
      for Me

and He arose from the place
and continued His journey
    toward Golgotha
        the place of the skull
      with His face set like flint
        with His eyes
           fixed
           on
           a tree
        in the form of a cross
           standing
           on the
           place
           of the
           skull

and as He continued that journey
Abraham's children
shouted after Him

crucify Him
crucify Him

how can they
change so quickly?

lamented an Angel

how soon they change
from worship
to ridicule
from praise
to condemnation
do they not know
their words
are a judgment
upon all
of Abraham's children?

and
almost
in
a blink
of their
eyes
                    the Angels watched
                    a struggle on Earth
                                as the Father of Heaven
                                    fought
                                    against Lucifer
                                for the deliverance
                                of all mankind
                                from sin
                                death
                                slavery
                                for dominion over
                                the entire Earth
                    so like the struggle
                    between Moses
                    and Pharaoh
                                for the deliverance
                                of Abraham's children
all of that struggle was focused on
                    the Son of Man
                    the Son of God
                    the Lamb of God
                        for His body
                            soul
                              spirit
                                as He
                                    hung
                                        on
                                        that
                                        tree

the Angels of Heaven
with tears in their eyes and hearts breaking
looked at the Son
hanging on that tree

how can the Father
allow this to happen
how can He love
them
so much
to withdraw
from His Son
and allow Him to suffer
and die on that tree?

in the other Heaven
the Angels of Darkness
rejoiced
laughed
celebrated

Lucifer's victory

it is his
the whole Earth
it belongs to Lucifer
Eve and her husband Adam
gave it to him
look at the Father's Son
submissive
without courage
unwilling to speak
even a word

we expected
more of a fight

Lucifer
               and many Angels
          of Darkness
               came down
                    to Golgotha
               and danced
          around the cross
     rejoicing
     singing

                              look at the Son
                              there He is
                              accursed
                              hanging
                              on that tree
                              we have won
                              we have won
                              victory

while they rejoiced
     the Son of Man
     the Lamb of God
     quietly whispered

                              Father
                              it is finished
                    I have done Your will
                         into Your hands
                    I commit My spirit

suddenly Lucifer
stopped rejoicing
     shouted
     angry

                         what is He doing?
                         why is it so dark?
               why is the Earth shaking?
               why are the graves opening?
               what are You doing Father?

and as he shouted
          the Earth shook
     even more
                and
Lucifer
                         began to
                    tremble
                              and the Angels
                                   of Darkness

                                   ran
                                        for

                                             cover

He died on that tree
the Prince of Peace
the Deliverer of the world
the King of Kings
the servant of all
the Son of God
the slaughtered Lamb
the Savior
of the whole Earth
of Adam's children

as they tearfully contemplated what was happening
one of the Angels whispered
hopeful

remember the words
of the lionkiller

why do the nations rage
and the people plot in vain?
the Kings of the Earth
take their stand
against the Lord
and His anointed
saying

let us break
their chains
and throw off their fetters

and the Father
scoffs at them
rebukes them
terrifies them
in His wrath

another Angel added

this is not the end
but the beginning
the Father's plan on Earth
will be fulfilled
death
will give way
to life
darkness
will change
to light

                                    despair
                                  will yield
                                  to victory
                              the Son of Man
                                will triumph
                                   in death

they buried Him
in a rich man's grave
this servant of all
        for three days He was in that grave
        for three days Lucifer rejoiced
              shouting

                                    it is mine
                                   I have won
                                  He was weak
                              this Son of God
                               look at Him now
                              defeated by death
                            where is your victory
                                     Father?
                               behold Your Son

finally
at the end of those three days
              the words of the Father
              came ringing from Heaven

                                 it is enough
                                 it is finished
                              You love me
                                   My Son
                             You have trusted Me
                           You have paid the price
                            You have set them free
                                come forth
                                   My Son
                                 in victory

the words the Father gave
to the lionkiller
rang throughout the Heavens
and shook the Earth

                        I have installed
                              My King
                              on Zion
                          My Holy Hill
                            You are
                            My Son
                today I have begotten You
                              ask of Me
                    and I will give You
                        the whole Earth
                      as Your possession

the Father proclaimed
lovingly

                          Son
                      come forth
                come out of the grave
                          death
                  you have no string
                          grave
                  you have no victory
                      come to me
                          Son
                    to My right hand
                    and rule with Me
                          forever

and the Angels of Heaven
praised the Father
glorified the Son

                as the resurrected Son
            and a multitude of captives
               delivered from captivity

    ascended to Heaven

                                        (to the
                                    right hand
                                        of the
                                    Father)

three
the Triumph of the Resurrected Son

at His crucifixion
His days in the grave
for days thereafter

        His disciples

        the ones He loved the most
        who followed Him
        who heard His words
        who shared His love for the Father

            scattered
                  in fear
         throughout
       Jerusalem

    even
    Peter
        the little rock
     a favorite disciple
        denied Him
            three
            times
          before He hung
            on that tree

but His special friend
the one He loved the most
His disciple
      John
   stood with His mother at the foot of the cross
     at the time of His crucifixion

He fixed His eyes on His mother
said to her

> Mother
> behold
> your son

He said to His beloved disciple

> John
> behold
> your mother

and from that day
         Mary

                   was a mother
                   to her new son John

         John

                   was a son
                   to his new mother Mary

         in a unity of spirit
         that only
         mother
         and
         son
         can experience

and after His death He found His disciples
and other followers
hiding from the authorities
near the bank of a sea

                        and He joined them there
                        and He watched them fish
                        and He ate fish with them
                        and He commissioned them to be
                        from that day forward
                        fishers of men

He turned to
Peter
the little rock
      and
      three
      times
      asked him

                      Peter
              do you love Me?

and in loving care
He fixed His eyes on
Peter
      as
      Peter
      three
      times
      cried
  (from the depths
    of His heart)

                       Yes
             I love You
                with all
              of my heart
             I love You
               You know
             I love You

and the Son of God
the Son of Man
the crucified one
        spoke to His friend
                        Peter
        with words of love
        that still ring
        in the Heavens

                                Peter
                        you love Me
                          I love you
                     you have denied Me
                   three times
                   and you have told Me
                   three times
                        you love Me

                        your body is weak
                        your heart is strong
                         I look at the heart
                           not the body
                        you will live for Me
                        you will die for Me
                           you are a rock
                           as I am the Rock

                        through My Spirit
                   you will speak words
                        you do not know
                   words that will ring
                           in Heaven
                           on Earth
                           forever

                        And it was so.

after
His death
His resurrection
His journey to Heaven

He returned once more
to His disciples
and spoke these words

gather together
in an upper room
to receive the Spirit
for you shall receive power
after Spirit is come
and you shall be My witnesses
to the ends of the Earth

and one hundred twenty
of His faithful believers
went to that upper room
where they met

Spirit

and they received from Him
a power
an anointing
that was to change
the whole world

and the Angels in Heaven watched
as this little group of Faithful believers

                              empowered from on High
                                    and by Spirit

went throughout Abraham's land
sharing their love

                                        for the Father
                                         for the Son
                                       for each other

        and even those
        who would not follow
        were heard to whisper

                        see how they love one another

                and one hundred twenty
                became three thousand
                and three thousand
                became five thousand

                              as the words of the Father
                                  spoken by the Son
                               repeated by the disciples
                        spread
        throughout

                                    Jerusalem
                Samaria
                        and other places
            on Earth

after His death
on that tree
    His days
    in the grave

                Son of God
                Son of Man
           Resurrected One

                          gathered from the grave
                         those who would follow
                              took them
                       to the right hand
                           of the Father

as the Angels of Light
looked at the Son
seated by the Father
looked at the faithful believers
struggling on Earth
        one of the Angels asked

                   why did He leave them?
                   why did He return
                       to the Father?

as they looked to Earth
        another Angel spoke

                        look at them
                    faithful believers
                       their nature
                   has not changed
               though they believe
                they are like Eve
                   like Adam
               after they ate
                 of that tree

while they watched
    their eyes
        fixed

           on a man
           traveling
              in
              Abraham's land

                this is
                Paul
          the twelfth disciple
              the one
                born
           out of season

said an Angel

          He will teach them
        the way to the Father

as he traveled
    this twelfth disciple
    spoke to all
    who would listen

           my brothers
            my sisters
           He is risen
          from the dead
          He lives in you
         you live in Him
          He is your life
         you are His life
        mind of His mind
       spirit of His Spirit
         life of His life

                                    but our nature
                                    has not changed
said a believer

                                    we still struggle
                                    to do the Father's will

                                    if you will live in Him
Paul answered

                                    you must die with Him
                                        your old life
                                    the Adam nature
                                            must die
                                        in order that
                                        your new man
                                    the nature of the Son
                                            will live

year
after
year
        as the Angels watched
                            this twelfth disciple
                    traveled
                                    from one city
                                        to another
        sharing with followers
        the glory of the Son

                        He is the image of the Father
                        the firstborn over creation
                        all things are of Him
                            made by Him
                                for Him
                        He holds everything together

157

of the followers
      this twelfth disciple proclaimed

                  we are His body
                  He is our head
                  our Bread of Life
                  the firstborn
                  from the dead
                  all His followers
                  dwell in Him

of the Father's plans
      he proclaimed

             we are reconciled to Him
             together with all things
             for in everything
             He is to have
             His supremacy

      and with
     Spirit
      standing at his side
       this twelfth disciple
        journeyed among them

        he drew to him those who were
              in distress
              sick
             discontent
             sinful
             without hope
        those rejected of men
        acquainted with grief

for he looked at their hearts
and not their bodies

             and most would not listen
            for they loved their traditions
         more than the glory of the Son of Man

until
this twelfth disciple

like the Son

was reviled of men
despised
rejected
cast into prison

from prison
with Spirit at his side
he prayed for each of them
cried out to the Father
with words that
rang in the Heavens
throughout the Earth
for all eternity

I pray the Father
will keep you
let it be
with wisdom
and revelation
may you know Him better
may your eyes be
enlightened
may your heart leap with
hope
may you know
of your calling
and of His greatness
may the same
life
of His life
power
of His glory
rule and reign in your lives

he cried out
for those who would follow

may they know
of His greatness
may they see Him
raised in glory
seated at the right hand
of the Father
in Heavenly realms
far above rulers
powers
and dominion
and every authority
of this place
named Terra
this place called Earth

and for this present age
and the ones to come
may we by His body
His fullness
fill the whole
Earth with His glory

from Heaven
the angels watched
this twelfth disciple

as he completed his journey
and poured out his life
for the love of the Father

and while they watched
    Spirit
    spoke

He was only a man
one solitary man
and his days were so few
walking with the Spirit
proclaiming the Father
glorifying the Son

yet his words
ring in the Heavens
and will be remembered
on Earth
they are words
of life and truth
like the words of the Son
that will ring
throughout eternity

one angel said
to another

see
what the Father can do
with one solitary man
truly committed to Him

but he is more than
a solitary
man

said Spirit

for he is a servant
of the Father
empowered by the Spirit
proclaiming the glory
of the Son

as the angels of light
looked to the Heavens
and joined in celestial praise
of the Father
and the Glory of the Son

they saw the Father
with the Son
seated at His right hand
high and exalted
in love and majesty

and the Father proclaimed

(to the Son
He loved
so much)

sit at My right hand
until Your enemies
are Your footstools
and I will extend
Your scepter
in the land of Your enemies
and Your brothers
Your sisters
those devoted to You
will be great warriors
arrayed in Your majesty
from the dawn of the day
until You see them
in Zion
Your Holy City

on the day of Your return

four
the Triumph
of the Church

and the disciples and other faithful believers
fought against Lucifer for the lives of all men
                                        women
                                        children
                    and for dominion of the entire Earth

in rapid succession the Angels watched
as they boldly proclaimed their faith
and Lucifer's servants rose up to persecute them
                                even burning them to death
but from their ashes
                    like a Phoenix
death gave way to life
and the death of one produced thousands
of faithful believers

the more they were persecuted the more their faith spread
and more faithful believers proclaimed the faith

and the Angels of Light heard from the other Heaven
        the defiant words of Lucifer
                                what is happening?
                        where do they get such courage?
                        why must they choose the Father?
                            why don't they follow me?
and finally
        in a quiet
        sinister
        voice
        Lucifer whispered

                                        I know
                            I will not fight them
                            I will join them

and in the passing of a moment in eternity
                                but decades and centuries on Earth
                    the Angels watched a little seed of faith
                            the size of a mustard seed
                        produced from the hearts of the faithful few
                                    grow into a giant tree

and it was different than any other tree
and its branches spread throughout the whole Earth
and its leaves were for the healing of the nations
and its fruit was food to the followers
                                nourishing all who would receive it

                    but this tree was so big
                    and its branches so large
                    that the birds of the air
                                    instruments of Lucifer
                    rested in its branches

for decades
and centuries
a millennium
and more
that giant tree
grew
        and grew

                                spreading its branches
                                over Earth

but as moments passed in eternity
few faithful ones
watered
cared
for that tree
and the leaves began to fall
and only a little fruit appeared on its branches

and the serpent
the one with Eve
with Adam
on that great day of choice
that same serpent
crawled around
under the branches of that giant tree
waiting
for men
women
children
to fall from its branches

that he might devour them
and there were many
who climbed on the tree
and played in its branches
but there were few
with their hearts
their minds
souls
spirit
who followed
the Son of God
the Son of Man

and cared for
that tree

and from the other Heaven
      Lucifer
      began to laugh
      and his angels shouted for joy
                    they say they follow you
                        Father
                but look at them now
                   like Adam
                     like Eve
                after they ate
                 of that tree

     one of the Angels of Light
     listening from Heaven
     began to lament
                  there is such darkness
                    down there
                       death
                    despair
                so much fighting
                done in the name
                  of the Father

     another Angel added
                their religious leaders
             those who follow the Son
              come near the Father
               with their mouths
                honor Him
                with their lips
                worship Him
           with their own traditions
              but their hearts
             are far from Him
            they have forgotten
         the sacrifice of the Son
      and do not know the Father
             or trust Him

but at the darkest hours
                    a man
                    a woman
                                        a remnant
            with the light
            of the Father
            shining brightly
            within
                        appeared on Earth
                        to do the Father's will
                        to proclaim the Father's words
                                                in spirit
                                                in truth
                to provide care
                and water
                for that tree

they were the faithful believers
        like Abraham
        like David
        like the twelfth disciple
                                        the one
                                borne out of season

but when one
        with the light of the Father
                began to shine
                        and to water
                        and care
                        for that tree

                            the birds of the air
                        resting in the branches
                                    of that tree
                            instruments of Lucifer
                    quickly devoured that one

            but as one was devoured
        another emerged
            with the light of the Father
                illuminating his way

            for there was always one

                        or there was always
                            a remnant

        to keep
        that tree
            alive

and finally
        a millennium
        and a half of a millennium
        and more
        passed on Earth

                        after the death
                     of the Son of Man

        with that giant tree

      spreading over all of Earth

            with few leaves

        little fruit

         and even less promise

as the Angels of Light
watched these things happen
      one of them proclaimed
                the Son created them
                  for the Father
                blood of His blood
                heart of His heart
                mind of His mind
                spirit of His spirit

                the Father chose them
                as His family
                the Father gave them
                dominion over Earth
                gave them the right
                to choose

He sent His Son
to live for them

they hung Him on a tree

the Son died for them
as the Lamb of God
to take away their sins

now only a remnant
follow the Son
and seek to do
the Father's will

they have taken
what He gave them
and have given it
to another

what more
could have been done
that was not already done?

finally

from the throne of the Father
in the Heaven of Heavens

came the words of the Father
spoken to Spirit

it is time
Spirit
today is the day of decision
now is the time of choice
go forth
my
Spirit
the wedding day approaches
gather those who will come
to our banquet table
as a bride
for my Son

and for me

a family

immediately
  the wind of

                      Spirit

                              began to blow
                              over the Earth

          first

                    as a gentle breeze
          then

                    as a mighty wind
                    shaking the branches
                    of that giant tree

            millions of Angels came from Heaven to Earth
              to aid the faithful believers as they gathered
                              those who would come
                          for the wedding of the Son

the faithful ones
traveled over Earth

                            to places of light
                            places of darkness
                            places
                            where they were welcome
                            places
                            where they were rejected

          and their voices
          spoken to the Father
          from Earth
          heard throughout all
          the Heavens
          as they cried out

                                        Father
                          give us the harvest
          and one cried

                              give me Scotland
                                  or I die

another cried

give me Wales
give us this nation
as one nation under God

throughout
the whole Earth

in places of light
and places of darkness
the faithful believers cried out

give us this land
Father
give us the people
let them be
a part of the Bride
and a part
of Your family

the Angels watched
the faithful believers

as they traveled
on foot
on donkeys
on horses

proclaiming the words

of the Father

telling

of the Son
and of His cross

gathering those
who would believe
as a part of
the Father's family

as the Angels of Heaven looked to Earth
                              they saw a struggle between
                              Father
                              Son
                              Spirit
                         and the faithful believers
                    fighting against Lucifer
        for the life of each man
                         woman
                         child
                                   who lived on Earth
the Angels watched
        as the faithful believers traveled to dark places on Earth
                         places where they had never been

and the lights of the lives of these faithful believers
began to shine in those dark places
                                   until Lucifer's servants
                         who held dominion over these dark places
                              put faithful believers to death

        but when the light of one faithful believer was put out

             thousands of lights
                                        the true light
                                        radiating
                                        from others
        appeared
                              until the darkness
                              gave way
                              to light

and one man
        woman
            child
                  after another
                                      died
                            as the Son had died

        with the light of their lives
        shining in the darkness
        and their voices
        ringing in the Heavens
                                Father
                        give us this land
                    as a part of the Bride

many faithful believers traveled to other places
that were not so dark
where they were free to travel
                        and they shared the words
                            of the Father
                          the crucifixion
                              of the Son
                        His resurrection
at first
        only a few people on Earth
        came to the giant tree
                      but as the faithful believers
                          traveled over Earth
            places of darkness
                became places of light
and thousands
                tens of thousands
      millions
                        tens of millions
         appeared in the branches
           of that giant tree

as the Angels looked down
they saw that giant tree
spreading its branches
over all of Earth

the birds of the air
instruments of Lucifer
still rested in its branches

and there remained
that group of believers
                           who sang
                                     and played
                       in that tree
            and waited
                          to go to the Father

but the faithful believers were there
                        to care for
                        and water
                        that tree

as the Angels looked
            they saw new leaves
               growing on its branches
                                 leaves
                       for healing of the nations
           and new fruit
      over all of that tree
                       fruit which was
                          the food of life
              for all
            who would eat it

and behind it they saw
the shadow of a cross
and a shadow
of that other
beautiful tree
the Tree of Life

finally
the whole Earth knew

of the Father
of the crucifixion
of the Son

and all men
women
children
on the whole Earth
came to a day of decision
and the time to choose

to choose light
to obey the words of the Father
to honor the Son
to experience the Light of Life

or to choose darkness
to follow Lucifer
and a day of judgment
instead of a wedding banquet

as they watched from Heaven
one of the Angels spoke

remember the words
of the prophet Joel
spoken in the days
of the Kings

multitudes, multitudes
in the valley of decision
for the day of the Lord is near
in the valley of decision

and the loving words
of the Father
rang from Heaven
throughout all of Earth

my Spirit
call them to Me
and to My Son
My Faithful believers
call them forth
from all of Earth
many will listen
but most will not
for most desire
darkness
judgment
death
and will not choose
light
salvation

and life

and the Father spoke
to the Faithful believers

(words that will be remembered
forever
and
forever)

the wedding banquet is ready
the day for the marriage of My Son
go to Jerusalem
to the nations
the uttermost places of Earth
go to the cities
to the street corners
the wilderness
invite to the banquet
the poor
the crippled
the blind
the lame
bring everyone
who will come
to the wedding of My Son

let them be

for My Son
a Bride
and for Me
a Family

And it was so.

five
the Triumphant Return

once again
the Angels looked to Terra (the place called Earth)
and as they watched, one believer and then another
proclaimed the words of the Father, the words of the Son,
and the teachings of Paul
and cried out to the Son in Heaven

> I died when You died
> I live in You
> My life is Your life
> I am one with You Lord Jesus
> and one with the Father
>
> look at those who understand
> such love of the Father
> such faithfulness to the Son

said an Angel

and as they looked, they saw something they had never seen
before, for these believers now lived in two places
they were seated with the Son at the right hand of the Father
sharing the joy of fellowship with the Father and the Son,
their voices ringing in Heaven

> teach us Father
> to do Your will
> share with us
> Your love, Your joy, Your truth

as the Father shared with them His heart, His nature
and His plans for man and for Earth

at the same time, these faithful believers walked the Earth
and their lives were not their own

                    but were the life of the Son –
for they had died and did not live except in the Son, and the
life each now lived was the resurrected life
                              of the Son of God
                              the Son of Man

and they cried out on Earth

                    we live in You, Son
                    our life is Your life
                    we are one with You
                    You are our health
                    our provision, our protection
                    we live in You

                    You are an ark
                    for our salvation, for our house
                    as You were an ark for Noah
                    in the day of the flood

and there were two groups of believers
that journeyed on Earth

there were those who believed,
but served the Father in their own strength
because their nature was the nature of Adam
these spent their days living in two worlds
one world was the world of Adam,
after Eve and her husband Adam ate of that tree
the other world was their new life
resting in the Son and His resurrection
and they never could decide
which world was their real home

but there was another group -- the true believers who
proclaimed their death with the Son and new life in Him

to this group, life was the unfolding of a great mystery,
as they lived their lives in the Son
at the right hand of the Father,
and as the Son lived His life in them
as they journeyed on Earth

over and over the true believers cried out

> You live
> in us
> Son
> Your life
> flows through our lives
> the lives we live
> we live in You

even though this group of true believers was small
their words, their lives, and the life of the Son living in them
radiated as the light of life throughout the whole Earth

for they were the true believers –
one with the Father, one with the Son,
bone of their bone, mind of their mind, spirit of their Spirit
and they were one with each other
for they were the Father's true Family

as they watched these two groups of believers
a wise Angel spoke

> it will be the same
> until the Son comes to Earth
> to take them to the Father

there will be many believers
most of them will never learn
to die to self
and to live in the Son

but the Father
loves them
and cares for them
as His Family

there will be those believers
the few who will unfold on Earth
the mystery of the crucifixion
and resurrection of the Son

and of their life in Him

as the Angels of Light looked to the throne of the Father
in the Heaven of Heavens
they heard the Son speaking to the Father

Father
take care of them
protect them
hear their prayers
use them to Your glory
lead them to Your glory

at another moment in eternity, the Angels assembled
with their eyes fixed on Terra, the place called Earth

Spirit spoke to them

the Son is prepared to go down there
the Marriage Day approaches
the Day of the Bride
the Day of the Gathering

will it be like the last time?
must He do that again?
will there be a second cross?

asked an Angel

this day will be different

replied Spirit

for this is the Day of Days
the Day of His Fullness
the Day of the Bride

and He has made peace
through His blood

a wise Angel responded

and He will reconcile
all things to Himself

said another

and another Angel proclaimed

remember the words of Isaiah --
the wolf will live with the lamb
and the leopard with the goat
and the calf with the lion

for He will make peace
with all things

said Spirit

and in Him
will all
be complete

at another moment in eternity, decades and centuries and
one millennium and almost another after
the resurrection of the Son,
the Angels of Light assembled in the Heavens in the presence
of the Father and the Son, and their eyes were fixed on Terra
(the place called Earth), and a special place called America

one of the Angels lamented
they all travel to and fro.
they go so fast from one place to another
they do not know where they are going
or what they will do when they get there.
they never stop to think of the Father, or the Son.
they think they have everything under control.
but they are lost, confused, without hope, without vision.

another Angel added
they have created such large cities!
their cities are places of rebellion, sin, violence --
like the city that Cain and his family built,
after Cain murdered his brother.
and even their children kill other children,
in the inner places of their cities.

another Angel added

and they even kill their own children --
millions and millions of their own children --
while they are still in their mothers' wombs.

and their governments are instruments
of deception and dishonor, and are not instruments of trust;
and the people think their leaders listen to them,
but they are manipulated and led like sheep --
like sheep to the slaughter.

another added

in early days, in America,
it was called one nation under God.
but now they do not permit
the name of the Father or the name of the Son
to be spoken, except in vain,
in places of government throughout America.

have they all turned away?
asked another Angel

then the Angels fixed their eyes on a man,
in a small city in the middle of America

he is an ordinary man.
said an Angel

there is nothing special about him,
nothing to cause one to notice.

except his desire.
added another

for he desires above all
a heart like David's heart,

and faith like Abraham's faith,
and to be an obedient servant,
like Moses was an obedient servant.

and that is why the Father loves him so much
added another angel
and he is one of many.
there are thousands, hundreds of thousands,
millions like him, living quietly,
but with desire brooding in their hearts,
and minds, and spirits.

these are the faithful believers.
added another Angel

and while the Angels watched this ordinary man
Spirit appeared at his side to comfort him,
and began to speak to him:

you are an ordinary man,
but extraordinary to the Father.
the world sees you as weak,
but the Father sees you as strong,
because the Father looks at the heart,
and not the body.

Spirit!

said the ordinary man

I want to know Him!
I want to know the Father!
I want to live in the Son,
and live in you, Spirit!
I want to live for the Father!

Spirit spoke to this ordinary man

>   the Father knew you before you were born.
>   and He called your name before creation,
>   before days began.
>   and He called you for this day.

> but how will I know when He is calling?
> >   asked the ordinary man
> how will I know the way He is leading?

>   the Father sent me to you.

said Spirit

>   I have taught you, and I led you,
>   even when you did not know I was leading.
>   You have learned more than most,
>   but less than many.

>   I will lead you, until the day
>   of the consummation of the Father's plan.

> What must I do?
> >   asked the ordinary man

>   Do not turn aside from the journey.
>   Do not turn to the left.
>   Do not turn to the right.
>   Set your face like flint
>   to do the Father's will.
>   Live in the Son, and He will live in you.
>   Call upon me, for I am
>   the sustaining power of your life.

Tell me of things to come.

                said the ordinary man

Tell me what will happen to America.

        It is not for you to know.

said Spirit

        To you it is a mystery,
until the Father chooses
to reveal His plan to you.

"But there are things the Father will reveal to you
in a glimpse and in a shadow"

"The whole Earth has yet to see," spoke Spirit, "what the Father can do when faithful believers -- ordinary men and women and children -- are wholly joined together as one, and fully consecrated to the Father"

As the Spirit spoke, the ordinary man saw a vision of the Earth, and he saw the fires of revival burning in one place and then another throughout the Earth -- a revival led by ordinary men with the fire of revival burning in their hearts.

And as the ordinary man watched, the flames of revival spread throughout the whole Earth, until all men, women, and children were forced to decide to follow the Son or to follow Lucifer.

"This is the day of decision. This is the time of choice,"
said Spirit.

"All men, and women, and children are in the valley of decision. Many will follow the Son, but most will not. For most will choose the way of Lucifer. Now watch closely and you will see, in a glimpse and a shadow,

what will happen on Earth."

And they watched, as Lucifer and his angels of darkness moved to and fro over all of the Earth -- and they made war against all men, women and children, but especially against Abraham's children.

All of Abraham's children, and all of the others on Earth, were brought to a place of decision -- to accept or deny the Son of Man, the Son of God, their Deliverer. Many chose to follow the Son, but most did not. But for those who chose to follow, a place was reserved in the presence of the Father, and the Son, and the Spirit

forever.

And then he saw a Holy City -- a New Jerusalem – descending from Heaven to Earth, a dwelling place for the Father and for the Son in this place named Terra, this place called

Earth.

(the Son was

                    the light
                    the life
                    the salvation
                    the provision

          for men
        for women
      for children

                    forever
                    and

                    forever)

And there
in the midst of the Holy City
was the Tree of Life
and its leaves
were for the healing
of the nations
and its fruit
was the food of life
for all men
and there were
no more tears
pain or suffering
for Adam's children

in the presence
of the Father
their sins
were washed away
by the blood
of the Lamb

for the Father
and the Son
now lived with man
forever and forever

And all the Angels in the Heavens of Heaven
rejoiced and praised the Father and the Son and the Spirit.
"And now we understand the love of the Father, the love of
the Son, the love of the Spirit," said an Angel, "and the
Father's plan for a bride for the Son, and for the Father a
Family." And as they looked to Terra, to the Holy City, they
saw a lion and a lamb, a leopard and a goat, lying together
under the branches of that beautiful tree. And while the
Angels rejoiced in Heaven, the Father spoke, and said,

"It is good.

Let it be."

(And it was so.)

contributors

Bill Hunter

is a practicing attorney with a keen sense of history. His first books, *God's Covenant With America* and *The Dawn of a New Day*, together constitute a two-volume study of American history from its early days to the present. Hunter has also studied Biblical history for most of his adult life. He believes the study of history is meaningful only by viewing the past from the perspective of the present, with a sense of God's unfolding plans for the future.

"Since God has given man a free will, the primary focus of history centers on the choices humans make, the consequences of those choices, and the manner in which God unfolds His plans within the framework of those choices. Central to any study of history is the life of Jesus Christ, the cross, and His resurrection. This book traces what I view as the defining events since creation, but it also anticipates God's unfolding plan for the gathering of the Bride for His Son and the consummation of the ages."

Michael Hunter

is a stage director and a writer. He received an MA in English Literature from the University of Edinburgh, Scotland. He is currently working on his PhD dissertation in Theatre at Stanford University, California, where he also teaches acting.

Charles Timothy Prutzer

officially began his career as a mural artist at the Denver Museum of Nature and Science in 1971. His murals are also in public and corporate collections, including the Denver Zoologic Foundation in Denver, Colorado; the Nature Conservation Department in Transvaal, South Africa; and the Rocky Mountain National Park.

His first and truest passion has always been more intimate paintings for private collections. These works have been shown in museums and exhibitions around the world, including the Beijing Natural History Museum, People's Republic of China; the Leigh Yawkey Woodson Art Museum, Wausau, Wisconsin; the Carnegie Museum of Natural History, Pittsburgh, Pennsylvania; the Museo Nacional de Ciencias Naturales in Madrid, Spain; and the Burrell Collection in Glasgow, Scotland.

Prutzer has been invited to work in several international wildlife projects. In 1994, he participated in the Artists for Nature Foundation's Expedition to Extremadura, Spain. He also went to India in 1997 as part of the Foundation's Project *Tiger Tiger* at the Bandhavgarh Nature Reserve.

His work has been published in *Best of Wildlife Art 2*, edited by Rachel Rubin Wolf, 1999; *Wildlife Art*, edited by Alan Singer, 1999; *Drawing and Painting Wildlife* by Edward Aldrich, 1998; and *Artists for Nature in Extremadura*, edited by Nicholas Hammond, 1995.

.

God's Covenant With America (Book 1) and *The Dawn of a New Day* (Book 2) are a history of America from a Christian perspective from its formative days up through the present. These books are also a passionate plea for the restoration of a Godly nation.

"I wrote this two-volume historical analysis of America because we can never understand America's present and future course without a clear understanding of our history, and we will never understand our history except through the light of God's divine plan and call for this nation." - Bill Hunter

Order these books at www.csnbooks.com/hunter or call toll free at (866)484-6184.

Hunter's e-mail address is hunters3@xit.net. Visit his website at www.billhunter.org.